Legs

How many legs
on a rabbit?
How many feet
on a mouse?
How many paws
on a puppy like yours
that scampers around the house?

Two on the table, two on the floor.
One, two, three, four!

Grandpa's Goldfish

Four little fish
in a bowl in the shop.
Three at the bottom, and
one at the top.

Tina's grandpa
bought four fish,
and carried them home
in a plastic dish.

'Those aren't goldfish,'
Tina said,
'One is orange, and
three are red.'

But, when they
swim in the lilypond
out in the sun,
there are splashes of gold
on every one!

Four in the Band

Four in the band
with a rum-te-tum-tum.
The first has a pipe,
and the second has a drum.

The third has a trumpet
blow, blow, blow!
And last comes the tambourine.
Away they go!

The Beehive

(Traditional)

Here is the beehive,
where are the bees?
Hidden away
where nobody sees.

Now they are flying
out of the hive.
One, two,
three, four, five!

Finger Painting

Four tall fingers,
and one short thumb.
Five altogether now,
here they come.

Five big blobs of
paint to spread.
Three are blue, and
two are red.

Over, under
the fingers swirl.
Up and down and
around they curl.

One, two, three, four,
five for a wash.
Into the water,
splishety, splosh.

Playtime

Out in the playground,
one on the swing.
Two on the see-saw,
three in a ring.

Four on the monkey-bar,
five on a log.
Six on the running-track.
Jog, jog, jog.

Six on the Trampoline

Six on the trampoline,
jump, jump, jump!
One bounced off, and
landed with a thump.

There were six at the start,
then one had a spill.
So, only five are jumping still.

Six on the trampoline,
jump, jump, jump!
Three bounced off, and
landed with a thump.

There were six at the start,
then three had a spill.
So, only three are jumping still.